Gary Glauber

The Covalence of Equanimity

SurVision Books

First published in 2020 by
SurVision Books
Dublin, Ireland
Reggio di Calabria, Italy
www.survisionmagazine.com

Copyright © Gary Glauber, 2020

Design © SurVision Books, 2020

ISBN: 978-1-912963-12-6

This book is in copyright. No part of this publication may be reproduced, stored in a retrieval system, or transmitted in any form or by any means without the prior permission in writing from the publisher.

Acknowledgments

Grateful acknowledgment is made to the editors of the following, in which some of these poems, or versions of them, originally appeared:

Chachalaca Review: "Atmosphere"

Foliate Oak Literary Magazine: "Summit"

Free Lit Magazine: "Compassion Fatigue"

KYSO Flash: "Save Your Pity," "Devotion," "Prevaricator," "A Capitol Idea," "Guidebook to Forgotten Places," and "The Sum of Three Parts During a Humdinger"

MacQueen's Quinterly: "Another Bad Year for Florida Man"

Misfit Magazine: "Alienating to Pleasure"

Mojave River Review: "The Lion Tamer's Nephew Doesn't Stand a Chance"

MonkeyBicycle: "Velvet Fog"

Pithead Chapel: "Preamble to the Theoretical"

Smokelong Quarterly: "How Pusch Came to Shovel"

SurVision: "Mariah"

Verse-Virtual: "Dear Board of Descriptors"

Contents

Devotion	5
Pet Peeve	6
The Lion Tamer's Nephew Doesn't Stand a Chance	8
Another Bad Year for Florida Man	10
Save Your Pity	13
Plankton	14
Mariah	17
Atmosphere	18
Velvet Fog	21
Prevaricator	22
Props to the Piece	23
Compassion Fatigue	24
A Capitol Idea	25
Summit	26
How Pusch Came to Shovel	28
Preamble to the Theoretical	30
Dear Board of Descriptors	31
Alienating to Pleasure	32
The Sum of Three Parts During a Humdinger	34
Guidebook to Forgotten Places	36
The Covalence of Equanimity	38

Devotion

Everyone here in the armory has the face of a peasant painted by Bruegel, and no one remembers how to smile. At the very least, the cold has masked many of the strong odors. Somewhere close a barking dog conducts a symphony of various sirens. This is city life, the opposite of silence, the nemesis of peace. I can't believe this is where she told me I could meet her parents. Right now, I feel as though I have time traveled to another century where I should protect myself from gypsies eager to separate me from my cherished belongings. I scan the great room and see nothing I recognize. I'm not even sure there's a way out, and when the gruff bearded man smelling of garlic approaches, I brace for the worst. He starts telling me about a timeshare in the Carpathian Mountains. I signal my need to be somewhere, anywhere else, immediately. My watch has stopped and my phone has lost power. She's still nowhere to be seen. I'm frustrated, but I realize this is as close to commitment as I've ever been. I stop and smile. So this is what they mean by love.

Pet Peeve

I was at home reading up on how the dark net was subverting our freedoms, when the phone rang. It was a woman from the local animal shelter.

"We have your Bootsie," she said. "Can you come down here and pick her up?"

I had no pets, but my curiosity got the best of me. I told her I'd be right there.

Bootsie turned out to be an adorable young feline, black with white markings on her lower paws, hence the name. Her tag did have my phone number on it. Perhaps the real owner never noticed the typo. Bootsie took an instant liking to me. She rubbed up against my pants leg and purred loudly. Her shaky tail clinched it. I signed the necessary papers and asked if I could borrow the carrier to transport her with me.

On the way home, I was taking extra care to go slowly, not hit any bumps or sharp turns that might upset my precious cargo. I must have been going suspiciously slow, as I now saw a cruiser's flashing lights urging me over to the nearby curb.

The officer asked for my license and registration. He looked in my window and saw Bootsie in the back.

"That your cat?" he asked.

"It would appear so," I said.

"I don't like your attitude," he said. "I'm going to have you take some tests."

"This is just great," I thought, as he went back to retrieve something from his vehicle, perhaps run a check on my plates and identification. I was expecting a breathalyzer, but instead he handed over a large stack of papers.

"I'm going to need you to try your best," he said.

Two hours later, the last circle on the scantron had been penciled in, and I handed it all back to the officer. He told me to wait in my car patiently.

He came back to my car after what seemed an awfully long time.

"I have some good news and some bad news," he said. "First, the good news. The University of Tallahassee is prepared to offer you a full scholarship to pursue a degree in electrical engineering."

This was a total surprise.

"However," he continued, "there are no pets allowed in the dormitories."

The Lion-Tamer's Nephew Doesn't Stand a Chance

It has never been a matter of money;
this is about taking risks,
putting your head directly
in the mouth of certain death and danger
while others look on in anxious anticipation,
hoping for the worst, but not admitting it.
This is the culture of modern expectation,
how so much happens so soon,
the young so much older than ever before.
Laughing wind sweeps sweat of quiet desperation
against loud aroma of cheap body spray.
This is the reckless abandoning
that follows our hero to the empty bleachers
as if he really had something important to say.
Already he regrets the supposition,
the underlying lie as lure
but she would not have come otherwise.
Laughing wind's chuckle confirms it.
She smiles, a picture of eloquent grace,
every movement a note in a larger symphony
playing to a packed heart.
She cannot be tamed,
yet sad nephew is happy
to breathe same air
of her steamed exhalations
on this chilled afternoon.
Pleading to please,
plotting to impress
via pregnant pause,

he stammers his statement,
invitation to a world of
shared experience, or at least to
a large coffee that he hopes
he can bring her tomorrow.
Sure, she says, a noncommittal
acquiescence, but to him
the equivalent of white tiger's
growled roar. As she gets up to leave
he hears imaginary crowd's gasps,
incredulously doubting
what has transpired
against tall odds.

Another Bad Year for Florida Man

It's become less a state and more a state of mind.
He wakes daily not knowing what perils will present themselves,
nor can he safely predict how he might react.
Life is unpredictable. That's his motto.
Will it be another python in the toilet?
That's not the best way to start out any day.
But he is brave, creative, a man who recognizes opportunity
and seeks to seize it in true *carpe diem* fashion.
Like the day when released from prison,
all those sweet late model cars tempting him
spot after spot in the jail parking lot. *What?*
In his defense, he only tried to steal 26 of them.
No one mentions all the ones left undisturbed.
He feels like a super hero,
because in a sense we're all super in some ways.
Besides, it's cool to dress as Spiderman
when power washing that Spanish-tiled roof.
People take notice, as well they should.
Because he is a hero at times:
fighting alligators to save his dog,
or pouring salt on the Walmart's floors
in order to remove evil spirits there.
See, he cares about others
and, like MacGyver, utilizes whatever is present
to solve pressing problems,
from pouring ketchup on his sleeping girlfriend,
to that time he attacked his own mother with a cob of corn.
Mostly, he is misunderstood.
That cocaine the cop found on his nose wasn't even his.
He tries to live a life of compassion and empathy.

When he broke into that elderly woman's home,
he wasn't there just to steal her belongings.
He also wore her clothes, trying to gain perspective,
walk a mile in her shoes, literally.
He is not a man of great skill or accomplishment,
asking a passerby to help start the scooter he wanted to steal,
or attempting to attack that ATM with a blowtorch.
They all seem like good ideas at the time.
Does any man deserve to be beaten up by the Easter bunny?
Life is unfair, even for a guy with deep authority issues.
He now knows telling the cops to go to Dunkin Donuts
was far better than the time he told them
he would behead them and eat their eyes and tongues.
It was a metaphor, perhaps. One that no one understood.
But all the great ones are that way.
Further, he is a freedom fighter, often going about his tasks
shirtless or completely naked. Feel the breeze. Open up.
It helps his basketball skills, he claims.
No one relates things in a fair and balanced way.
That time he fought a tree, did anyone mention
how the tree was the one that started it?
Or when he attacked that mattress – did anyone realize
that mattress was where his girlfriend's lover had been hiding?
He is a victim of incomplete and subjective reporting.
They never tell the full story.
Does he have anger issues? Doesn't everyone?
Perhaps he overreacted when stabbing his nephew
for taking too long in the bathroom.
In hindsight, that seems obvious.
Or when he threatened the handyman with the sword
just because the power outage ruined his video console.
Or when he beat up his folks over that acidic pork chop.
He promises to work on the anger thing.

This year will be different, he swears,
a new start and some practical resolutions:
no firing the gun inside the house,
no stealing boxes of golf balls stuffed down his pants,
no pooping in the yard,
no power washing his neighbors.
This year he'll finally disband his army of turtles.
He'll remember to wear clothes when visiting the mall,
and try to not burn down the house
baking cookies on the George Foreman grill.
It's the thought that counts, he tells me,
even when the road back to jail
is paved with good intentions.

Save Your Pity

She reserves her scorn for those in power who have made poor choices; she has been there before, when ruling over the kingdom in that famous underwater city, back when arts were supported and lungs could go water or air. Back then, technology had rid us of illness, perfecting this human journey, back before the alien overlords packed up and took with them the cures. She blames herself, knowing her brand of sarcasm doesn't always sit well with extra-terrestrial intelligences, those big heads and serious eyes, no real sense of humor or irony. There's not much humor in being probed; like a stick in someone's eye, people get hurt. That explains a lot, with karma placing her this lifetime in Nutley, NJ, working part-time as a cashier in a warehouse/grocery store. So when espying the pretty celebrities that fill her tabloid rack, she doesn't really feel jealousy or compassion. They know the deal, she figures. They knew it from long before the paparazzi started snapping candids. This is the fate they've signed on for, the deal that puts them in the miserable one percent, far above the fray and yet caught up in their personal sacrifices, signing off on privacy to let the populous have their vicarious jollies. Beware the common envy. She shakes her head knowingly.

Plankton

Loss is a robe dripping water,
murky undertow hiding it.
Invisible heartbeats keep rhythm
against dangerous refrain:
thousands abandoned, fathoms deep,
and more falling, unfathomable.

The insect is a grid of eyes watching,
indicting, inviting guilt in regret's fine home,
this manor of secrets with defensive walls
sterilized for your protection.
The what-if turns into a state of because:
reasons, factors, qualified always
to express simplicity of failure,
enormity of loss.

The anesthesia was quite pleasant,
invoking dreams of bygone days
in a cavern of seaside happiness,
a place for well-decorated hibernation.
In the distance, rattles of mercy buzzed
raucous chorus below cerulean blue.
This is the window of opportunity,
but look before leaping, for
a mind is terrible to waste.

You awaken alone in a room of strangers,
thin curtains instead of privacy,
a greeting card without a message.

How do we track the next incarnation?
You almost recognize your own voice.
Machines have wires that grid you,
mapping trauma body has suffered.
Readouts and beeps are hallelujahs.
Can I still get a rousing amen?

The ocean is full of slimy dark mysteries
and each depth grows darker still.
Creatures are abominations of ugliness,
seemingly nature's cruel jokes,
more celestial mistakes without reason.
There are no answers here, just distant
whale moan of misery and forfeiture,
a horrible dirge with krill for dessert.
Schools of strange fish swim by,
with eyes that judge, silently.

Tides are mood shifts, lunar
ebb and flow of saline waves,
tears and backwash on a global scale.
The susurrus of lost souls
wake Neptune from his brief slumbers
and start him rowing toward underworld.

You wring robe and try to walk steadily
out beyond nearby shoals.
Crashing sounds growing louder
as other voices fade: doctors, nurses, priests.
Absence obtains presence and sun still rises.
Twenty leagues beneath this beach

a crab crawls sideways with purpose,
living proof that this world allows
those who hide in shells to slowly,
warily emerge.

Mariah

What a windy world you have here.
She says her home is nothing like it.
Our branches never tremble and bend.

They jounce the way a belly shakes
from laughter, the way a chipmunk
scurries with tail up across dirt road.

We love the wind, he tells her.
It is the breath of gods, reminding
how so much is beyond our control.

It whistles in a haunting way, as if
to stir the dead from their graves.
I had better hold you closer, she says.

And as he watches rickety contraption
hold fast against near gale forces,
he embraces her embrace in silent thanks
to invisible things uniting them.

Atmosphere

I.

One who identifies far outside gender
and has made a career of celebrating
a terrorized and broken past
has put me in charge of greeting
the vast feted guest list of artistes
and guileless saboteurs, gathered
to yell guttural phrases against
a darkened backdrop of museum
castoffs, meaning as sound,
masquerading too hard as art,
and inviting mute applause.

This is captured moment as story,
the morning-glory of fresh growth
in vases stale with vape juice.
We are ornaments of torments,
silly fools and charlatan renegades,
goth devotees of binge-watched culture
beautifully alone and ironically attractive,
hypersensitive to touch and yet
braying out prayers for organs
and grinders, harsher reminders
of how skin becomes payback
in patriarchal dissolution
where power no longer
invites sad compliance.

II.

It's all a new science,
cooled and rewired
and somewhat admired:
handshakes replacing
neural connection,
in avant garde haunting,
echoes in hipster enclave.

III.

Let pity compel you
by what strangers tell you,
this city will fell you
if given a chance.

Shrieks meant to savor
cannot save behavior,
we act like cold neighbors
refusing to dance.

IV.

Those off beat mountebanks
form their own stale rhythms
in the spirit of performance,
yet this throbbing steady pulse
is a techno headache
even Warhol could not redeem.

V.

Another arrives:
dutifully, I check the list.

Velvet Fog

I called forensics again. They hung up. If I can't get justice, at least give me results. I don't ask for much, maybe some DNA testing. At the very least, they should have done something with that pile on the sofa.

"No, Mr. Wendersby," they tell me the first few times. "We're a local police department, we don't do such things. We're not a CSI television show."

For their information, I don't even watch television. Rather than tell me anything, they ask me to stop calling. It's a world gone crazy, where age counts for nothing.

Tuesday it happened. Got myself a nice lump on the head, thank you. They came, two of them, knocked me out cold with some heavy object, the butt of a revolver, I don't know. Something.

When I come to, I look to see what's missing. I'm not rich; I live a fairly spartan existence. They seem to have taken only my Mel Torme albums.

When I tell the sergeant, I see the smirk on his face. He doesn't believe me, nor does his sidekick, Officer Peachfuzz fresh out of the academy. I may be old, but I'm not about to start pooping on my own furniture. Even with a faulty memory, I still have my pride.

Prevaricator

Everyone assumed Ben's older brother was the big expert. When he told me that, by touching Geraldine's freckles in a way that resembled a constellation, she would give in to my every request, I believed it. I found out the hard way it wasn't quite gospel. He claimed his poodle was part wolf. "Listen to its bark," he advised. "That's where it becomes obvious." There was an endless stream of these gems. Yet he could really put it across. Most were convinced. He was good at lying. I believed him when he said he saw our kindergarten teacher naked. "People have to be naked at least once a day," he said. "And my brother has a friend who has a window across from her apartment." Nothing could ever be substantiated. Lie upon lie, a deluge of confabulated delusion. I heard he became a successful lawyer. If you can make others believe, there's a place for you in this crazy world.

Props to the Piece

This hectic turn of hellbent troll,
His hillocked highway burning soul,
as willy and nilly take the boards,
he flutters shutters with windy accords.

A snuffling tough flashes urban cachet,
while spraying up courtsides with neon array,
proclaiming his tag, his discontent showing,
a few zigs and zags, soon the art begins flowing.

All dappled with drowsy, his lids start to close,
obscene dreams of power turn all purple prose
to simple accessible feelings of reflex,
three farthingstone's distance from street level defects.

Three numbers, three letters, impossibly high:
bombing in bubble speak, King Krylon fly,
burning the landscape of train, bridge, and sign,
conflating the stating "what was yours is mine."

Compassion Fatigue

Welcome to the post-truth era
where deceptive illusion blurs
into semblance of semi-genuine
and news is cheap and plentiful,
a ceaseless bounty that exhausts
and plagues overtaxed brain.
This avalanche of endless chaotic chatter
has worn out two thirds of the populace,
its drivel of headline noise and nonsense,
overwhelm of overload, point of pointless
saturation left long ago in distant rearview,
where information may appear larger
or truer than it really is – hindsight
and foresight newly interchangeable,
panels of so-called experts yelling
to get their Warholian fifteen across in five.
Alleged facts fly fast and loose,
essential questions go unanswered
by outspoken all out and speaking,
tweeting, talking points poking viewers
in uncomfortable ways, cycle after cycle,
as breaking news becomes forever broken
and Leary's chant takes on new meaning
for a media-plagued generation eager to
"turn on, tune in, then drop out."

A Capitol Idea

To save his marriage, he agreed to take her to the Capitol. But something happened along the way. They took Amtrak, but when they emerged from the tunnel, the world had changed. Things were askew. The sidewalks didn't quite match up with any concept of parallels, and every day at four there was a short but violent thunderstorm. It was in The Museum of Unfortunate Seats when he began to take notice. He moved into the room where there was a recreation of the president's row from the Ford Theatre, and before you could say John Wilkes Booth, he noticed his wife was growing younger. Her hair was longer; her dimple looked fetching for the first time in years. Later that day, after a short stop at The Museum for Postage Stamps of FBI Cases, he confronted her with this finding. "Seeing all these important things makes me feel like a little girl again," she said. "Can we go to this tomorrow?" She handed him a brochure from the hotel rack: it was the grand opening of a show in the former emergency room of George Washington University Hospital – *The Womb of the Unknown Soldier*. He wasn't thrilled by the idea, but her enthusiasm won him over. Besides, the pamphlet stated the 3-D surround sound virtual reality show was "a life-changing experience." The loud boom startled him and the pouring rain followed soon after. "Must be four," he said, but when he checked his wrist, the watch was missing.

Summit

They stand at the precipice,
looking out, looking down,
looking good while checking out
vast panorama that lies before them.
It's a long drop, a dare,
a taunt of possibility.
You only reach the summit once
and the feeling of invincibility
dominates like expert magic.
No one cites good health,
muscle tone, the absolute control
over deceptive young body,
nor its inherent beauty.
That's unstated given,
starting point from which
real transformation begins.
Second journey commences:
first tattoo, some paid-for pain
into irreversible decision;
glass of wine or three,
surreptitious venture
into social drinking,
ignoring family history,
violent alcoholic
father, uncle, mother, friend;
toying with needle or pill
or gender exploration
of playful kisses and touching,
pretending to understand
real wants and needs.

They look so grown up.
Advice the wind proffers
says look long before leaping
but they do not hear it,
they do not heed it.
Every generation needs
mistakes of their own,
so if they survive them
they'll later come whispering
wisdom to ones that follow,
holding collective breath
as next group inches closer
to the cliff edge of change.

How Pusch Came To Shovel

John Pusch Jr. had few real regrets, but seeing how his major in philosophy had little practical application in the real world oft proved daunting. Thoughts of easier choices could inspire pointless envy, true tales of those less capable from an intellectual standpoint now handsomely remunerated, firmly ensconced in cherry-wood paneled offices high over the city, transformed by time and money and paper into semi-respected lawyers and businessmen. But Pusch lacked pull.

Once he had tested patience by temping in such places. That test proved troublesome, gargantuan efforts expended to keep comments unspoken for miniscule wages, insubordination bubbling just beneath the surface, followed by violent dreams of vengeance.

Bereft of choices, he spent time in meditation, quizzing his higher self to point the way. The spirit guides kept their learned silence. Bills had to be paid, and there was no way he could tolerate overpaid baboons. "I will dig and dig until I find an answer," he said, and realized he already had stated his solution.

So here he was, like a child again, shovel in hand. Digging was hearty outdoor activity, allowing his mind free realm while the body went about its appointed task, vigor renewed, blood flowing, a feeling of general health in spite of the occasional blister. The ground a worthy opponent, often hiding roots and rocks that held their own against the steel edges, hampering what otherwise was a fairly simple activity.

This brisk time of year, he noted, you often had to give your all. The hard-packed surface of what had once been sod cover, now fodder for the shovel's restless appetite. As winds provided a whistling soundtrack to his strenuous efforts, he knew the key was to continue on. The earthy smell of the freshly turned soil scented the chill breeze and urged him forward. Aches and pains could wait for later; he was lost in the action itself: one man, one goal, one hole.

Preamble to the Theoretical

I am here to import your novelties, I told them. They buzzed me in. The elevator was old and slow and rickety, but I never expected anything else. This whole building was dark stairwells and danger warnings. The sun never made it indoors. I had to push the door open against a pile of string spooled across the factory floor. Show me your best, I told them. They gave me the gorilla suit and I ran with it, knowing it would always have a place in our catalog. Neither trendy nor overly clever, it still spoke to a history of the species, and there was wry irony in knowing it would evolve over time.

Dear Board of Descriptors

In reference to your recent cease and desist missive
regarding said terms *sexy* and *inviting*, I regretfully
offer my compliance, noting the unlikely scenario
when either of these might find their way
into any salvo of normal casual conversation.
As the years go by, and my hair turns thinner and grayer,
smiles of flirtation transform to smirks
of kindly tolerance, the kind of grandfatherly
wisdom that says a nod is the latter day equivalent
of a *come hither* wink, and the ego thrives yet
on the idea of an older, distinguished presence
as handsome, beguiling, rather than worrying
about some errant stain or food stuck in teeth surprises.
Aging is a process of gaining solitude and your curb
on acceptable terms helps ease that slow cruise
into eventual silence where *sexy* and *inviting*
used to live alongside moxie, panache, and razzamatazz.

Alienating to Pleasure

The attractive woman's picture
appeared onscreen, smiling.
It was no name I recognized,
and the face rang no bells either.
"Good evening, how are you?"
she began innocently enough-
but this was not my first
online rodeo.

You see the warning signs.
She's a nurse or a missionary
doing work in Western Africa.
She's a member of the armed forces.
She's a former model looking
for new friends.

No thanks.

There's an awkward
whiff of illegitimacy
that sours such exchanges.
Who is on the other side?
Savvy hacker, some
foreign scammer
out to lure and catfish,
reel in the unsuspecting
with the bait of physical wiles?

Again, not interested.

She continued in a way
that exposed her lack
of mastery in English.
"I would like to apologize
for the inconvenience,
but I would like to meet you
if you do not find this
alienating to pleasure."

No time, no interest,
I ignored the message.
If she was real,
I'll never know.
But is it wrong
to still feel flattered?

The Sum of Three Parts During a Humdinger

I was a bit-part actor in someone else's grand play
and it was hotter than tarnation that summer.
I was tutoring the button maker's three daughters
when they decided to go all 23 skidoo on me,
knowing I could only chase in one direction.
With two missing teens, my best guess was
the local Cone-a-rama, where their penchant
for soft serve might have led them. They
also were hot to trot for the neighbor's son,
so I tried there first. Turns out he was away
at camp. The one daughter in tow refused
to tell me where I might find her sisters,
serving up some fancy applesauce she thought
I might fall for. I didn't. Instead we headed over
to the local park's gazebo, where rehearsals were
underway for some Brodie of a summerstock
production. I found the two fugitives there,
outfitted in odd period regalia for a duo dumb act,
spouting the wisdom, "There's no mime
like the present." I failed to see the humor
in their awkward charade, and after extending
apologies to Ms. Witherspoon, the librarian
heading these ragtag thespians, I made them
change and return to our algebra lesson, with
a mind to report this to The Gerry Society.
They said theater was in their blood, and
I countered with a plea for a more practical
transfusion. Their banter was amusing, but

I wasn't about to tell them that. I was a constant being multiplied by their variables, and unless they began some coefficiency soon, everything would turn irrational and I wouldn't get paid.

Guidebook to Forgotten Places

(from page 59)

That place beneath the bleachers where that girl Jan allowed you to touch her breasts. You kissed her hard because you hardly knew her, and she let you because she was a clarinet-playing band geek who would not realize her own beauty until maybe four years later, ironically, at a Catholic college in Boston. You remember being thrilled and delighted by the experience, yet you never called her again, and managed to avoid her in the high school's hallways. Those bleachers were eventually deemed unsafe and replaced by ones that provided no underneath access.

(from page 167)

That poorly lighted pub in the small main street of that little town in Scotland, where you hitchhiked that time. There was that fascinating blonde woman playing footsie with you beneath the crowded table, playing it perfectly straight-faced the whole time, right up until she handed you that paper with her name and number, and gave you a kiss out back where no one could see and you swore you would always remember that night. You carried that paper around in your wallet for five years, proof that the impossible does occur.

(from page 293)

That old discount mall, anchored by a cheap liquor store. There were various no-name stores that offered bounteous bins of clothes at off-rate prices. Much of the mall's wares seemed picked-over, as did the place itself. It was always busy with folks eager for bargains, crowds of strange ethnicities, from Eastern European extreme religious sects to hordes of various Asians, all gathered in unity for what could be had for less. There was a roomful of colored balls where parents would drop off their kids for birthday parties. Once one of your own kids would actually go missing in that mall for a seemingly eternal ten-minute stretch. They found him hiding inside a display rack of discount skirts, blissfully unaware of the anxiety he caused. That mall has since been razed and replaced by a Target.

The Covalence of Equanimity

(An Epithalamion)

Sure, it's a world beset with horrible woes,
and each ensuing day triggers additional concerns –
we know. We watch the news, fake and otherwise.
But there is a remedy. Proven, reliable,
guided by fate and providence. A wise solution
for those lucky enough to capture lightning
in a life-shaped bottle and tell the tale after.
I am one such survivor, so listen carefully.
Know that two is far more than the sum of
its individual parts, exponentially, vastly more,
that a coordinated unity unleashes an ability
to slay challenges, to tame an unruly world,
to find laughter and light through a bond of love.
It makes little sense – but it's been proven
through historic annals of time and being.
The power of two-as-one is mighty and
can be mighty fun. So gather ye rosebuds
as you hear time's winged chariot approach
and rejoice in the sharing of experiences,
of memories made and moments enriched
through that very condition, for life is meant
to be shared and appreciated together.
This hard to find covalence of equanimity
is simple when discovered – the peaceful
sharing of love is how you tolerate, remediate,
nay celebrate this absurd blessing called life.

So couple, use this power well, explore
how life shared in love transcends limitation,
offering immortality rooted in tradition,
a happiness emanating as inspiration
from sharing this powerful two-as-one condition.

More poetry published by SurVision Books

Noelle Kocot. *Humanity*
(New Poetics: USA)
ISBN 978-1-9995903-0-7

Ciaran O'Driscoll. *The Speaking Trees*
(New Poetics: Ireland)
ISBN 978-1-9995903-1-4

Helen Ivory. *Maps of the Abandoned City*
(New Poetics: England)
ISBN 978-1-912963-04-1

Elin O'Hara Slavick. *Cameramouth*
(New Poetics: USA)
ISBN 978-1-9995903-4-5

John W. Sexton. *Inverted Night*
(New Poetics: Ireland)
ISBN 978-1-912963-05-8

Afric McGlinchey. *Invisible Insane*
(New Poetics: Ireland)
ISBN 978-1-9995903-3-8

Anatoly Kudryavitsky. *Stowaway*
(New Poetics: Ireland)
ISBN 978-1-9995903-2-1

Tim Murphy. *The Cacti Do Not Move*
(New Poetics: Ireland)
ISBN 978-1-912963-07-2

Tony Kitt. *The Magic Phlute*
  (New Poetics: Ireland)
  ISBN 978-1-912963-08-9

Clayre Benzadón. *Liminal Zenith*
  (New Poetics: USA)
  ISBN 978-1-912963-11-9

George Kalamaras. *That Moment of Wept*
  ISBN 978-1-9995903-7-6

Anton Yakovlev. *Chronos Dines Alone*
  (Winner of James Tate Poetry Prize 2018)
  ISBN 978-1-912963-01-0

Bob Lucky. *Conversation Starters in a Language No One Speaks*
  (Winner of James Tate Poetry Prize 2018)
  ISBN 978-1-912963-00-3

Christopher Prewitt. *Paradise Hammer*
  (Winner of James Tate Poetry Prize 2018)
  ISBN 978-1-9995903-9-0

Mikko Harvey & Jake Bauer. *Idaho Falls*
  (Winner of James Tate Poetry Prize 2018)
  ISBN 978-1-912963-02-7

Tony Bailie. *Mountain Under Heaven*
  (Winner of James Tate Poetry Prize 2019)
  ISBN 978-1-912963-09-6

Nicholas Alexander Hayes. *Amorphous Organics*
  (Winner of James Tate Poetry Prize 2019)
  ISBN 978-1-912963-10-2

Maria Grazia Calandrone. *Fossils*
  Translated from Italian
  (New Poetics: Italy)
  ISBN 978-1-9995903-6-9

Sergey Biryukov. *Transformations*
  Translated from Russian
  (New Poetics: Russia)
  ISBN 978-1-9995903-5-2

Alexander Korotko. *Irrazionalismo*
  Translated from Russian
  (New Poetics: Ukraine)
  ISBN 978-1-912963-06-5

Anton G. Leitner. *Selected Poems 1981–2015*
  Translated from German
  ISBN 978-1-9995903-8-3

All our books are available to order via
http://survisionmagazine.com/books.htm